CONTENTS

Scan QR codes throughout for step-by-step pictures of each craft.

TECHNOLOGY

What can you make with old headphones and recycled cardboard and plastic? Tech crafts! Revamp or repair old devices with a little creativity. This saves technology from the landfill. Save other materials from the landfill too by repurposing them into working devices or cool device accessories!

Get ready to create Earth-friendly technology!

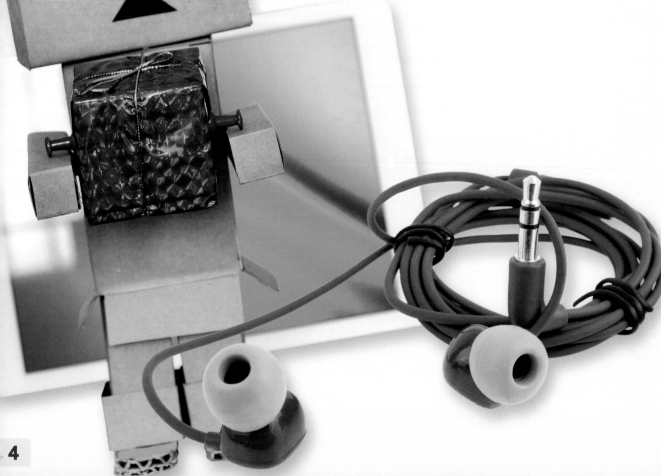

Green STEAM

EARTH-FRIENDLY
TECH
CRAFTS

Veronica Thompson

Lerner Publications ◆ Minneapolis

Lerner Publications Company
A division of Lerner Publishing Group, Inc.
241 First Avenue North
Minneapolis, MN 55401 USA

For reading levels and more information, look up this title at www.lernerbooks.com.

Main body text set in Avenir LT Pro 12/16.
Typeface provided by Linotype AG.

Photo Acknowledgments
The images in this book are used with the permission of: © cosmaa/Shutterstock Images, p. 1 (Earth icon); © Stilesta/Shutterstock Images, pp. 1, 3, 9, 11, 13, 15, 17, 19, 21, 23, 24, 25, 27, 28 (border design element); © Etienne Hartjes/Shutterstock Images, p. 4 (robot); © vincent noel/Shutterstock Images, p. 4 (earbuds); © Paolo De Gasperis/Shutterstock Images, p. 5; © Patnaree Asavacharanitich/Shutterstock Images, p. 6 (dishes); © republica/iStockphoto, p. 6 (waste basket); © Stephen VanHorn/Shutterstock Images, p. 6 (jar); © Barcin/iStockphoto, p. 7; Veronica Thompson, pp. 8, 9 (top), 9 (center), 9 (bottom), 10, 11 (top), 11 (center), 11 (bottom), 12, 13 (top), 13 (center), 13 (bottom), 14, 15 (top), 15 (center), 15 (bottom), 16, 17 (top), 17 (center), 17 (bottom), 18, 19 (top), 19 (center), 19 (bottom), 20, 21 (top), 21 (center), 21 (bottom), 22, 23 (top), 23 (center), 23 (bottom), 24 (top), 24 (bottom), 25 (top), 25 (bottom), 26, 27 (top), 27 (center), 27 (bottom), 28 (top), 28 (center), 28 (bottom); © Curly Pat/Shutterstock Images, pp. 9, 11, 13, 15, 17, 19, 21, 23, 24, 25, 27, 28 (design element); © chaythawin/Shutterstock Images, p. 29 (right); © eelnosiva/Shutterstock Images, p. 29 (left); © tentor/Shutterstock Images, p. 30; © pagadesign/iStockphoto, p. 31; © Liza2017/Shutterstock Images, p. 32 (top); Courtesy Veronica Thompson, p. 32 (bottom).

Front cover: Veronica Thompson (main); © cosmaa/Shutterstock Images (Earth icon)
Back cover: © Curly Pat/Shutterstock Images (background design element); © Stilesta/Shutterstock Images (border design element)

Library of Congress Cataloging-in-Publication Data

The Cataloging-in-Publication Data for *Earth-Friendly Tech Crafts* is on file at the Library of Congress.
978-1-5415-2417-0 (lib. bdg.)
978-1-5415-2783-6 (pbk.)
978-1-5415-2422-4 (eb pdf)

Manufactured in the United States of America
1-44505-34761-5/1/2018

CHOOSING MATERIALS

When you're gathering items to repurpose, it's okay to be picky. For example, avoid cardboard with food or grease stains on it. And ask an adult for permission before working with old or broken electronics.

CLEAN MACHINE

Reused materials may carry food or leftover substances. Give these materials a good scrub before crafting with them! Rinse and dry empty plastic containers. And have an adult help you wash and dry used clothing items.

STAY SAFE!

Some crafts in this book require sharp or hot tools. Ask for an adult's help when using these items:

- craft knife
- hot glue gun
- large knife

ROBOT EARBUD CASE

Turn an old container into a tiny robot to hold your earbuds! A waterproof case will help protect the wires from wear and tangling when not in use.

MATERIALS
~ small recycled plastic candy
   container with lid
~ paint
~ paintbrushes
~ glue
~ beads
~ clear nail polish

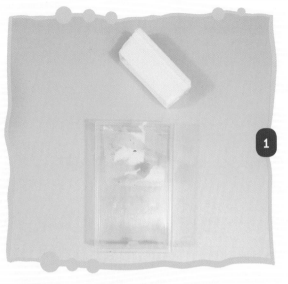

1 Remove any labels from the container. Then remove the lid to prevent painting it closed.

2 Paint the container to look like a robot.

3 Glue some beads on the container as robot buttons.

4 Allow the paint to dry. Then coat the container in clear nail polish. This will help the paint stay on longer. Let the nail polish dry.

5 Roll up your earbuds and place them inside the robot. Pop the container lid back on and safely carry your earbuds in a pocket or backpack!

SWAP IT!

The small candy container could be replaced with an empty plastic spice bottle or gum container.

Scan the QR code for more photos.

STRING·LIGHT SIGN

Give wrapping paper and old string lights a new purpose in a glowing sign!

STEM Takeaway
Electric current travels through wire in plugged-in string lights. The wire serves as a conductor.

MATERIALS
~ old string lights
~ thin recycled cardboard
~ scissors
~ sharpened pencil
~ thick recycled cardboard
~ recycled twist ties
~ leftover wrapping paper

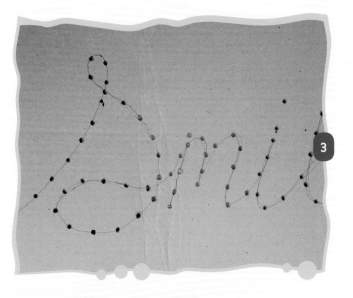

1 Plug in your lights to test them. But it's okay if a few bulbs are burned out or dim!

2 Cut a large rectangle of thin cardboard. Draw a word or design on it.

3 Protect your work surface with a layer of thick cardboard. Have an adult help you use a sharpened pencil to punch holes in the thin cardboard along the design. Make each hole about 1 inch (2.5 cm) apart.

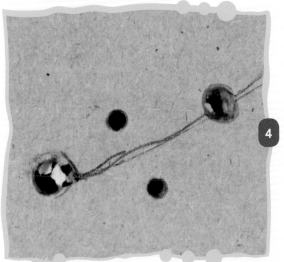

4 Punch two smaller holes near the first and last holes in your design. Thread one twist-tie through each set of smaller holes, and twist its ends together at the back of the cardboard.

5 Cut a piece of wrapping paper a bit larger than the cardboard. Lay the design facedown on it. Fold over and tape down the paper edges.

6 Working from the back of the cardboard, gently re-poke each hole through the paper. Gather the lights and pop one into each hole. Tape any extra length to the cardboard.

7 Open and reconnect the twist-ties around the string to help hold it in place. Finally, plug in your work of art!

CELL PHONE CRADLE

Transform a recycled container into a colorful cradle that will hang a cell phone on an outlet as it charges!

MATERIALS
~ small recycled plastic container, such as a shampoo bottle
~ cell phone
~ marker
~ craft knife
~ cell phone charger and power adapter
~ scissors
~ washi tape
~ paint
~ paintbrushes

STEM Takeaway

Many cell phone chargers work by sending pulses of electricity from an outlet to a cell phone battery. This recharges the battery's power!

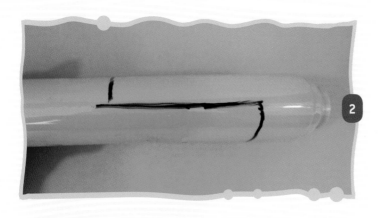

1 Make sure the plastic container is slightly wider and much taller than the cell phone. Remove any labels from the container.

2 Draw a horizontal line across the front middle of the container. On the back, draw another line just under the top of the container. Then, on both sides, draw a vertical line connecting the front and back lines.

3 With an adult's help, cut along the lines. Start the cuts using a craft knife. Complete them using scissors. Recycle the top portion of the container.

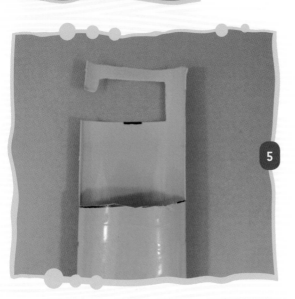

4 Place your phone inside the container and set the phone charger power adapter above the phone. Hold the adapter in place while you remove the phone from the container. Then outline the adapter in tape. Extend the bottom line to the edge of the container. Remove the adapter.

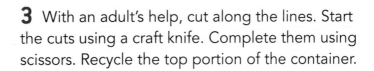

5 Cut out inside the tape shape from step 4, but leave a small hook in the top corner of the cutout. Remove the tape.

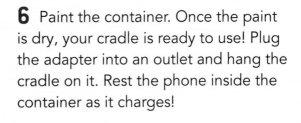

6 Paint the container. Once the paint is dry, your cradle is ready to use! Plug the adapter into an outlet and hang the cradle on it. Rest the phone inside the container as it charges!

CORK COMPASS

A compass helps people navigate. But you don't need to buy one! Make your own from repurposed household items.

MATERIALS
- recycled plastic food container
- craft knife
- scissors
- recycled cork
- large knife
- cutting board
- sewing needle
- refrigerator magnet
- water

STEM Takeaway
Earth has a magnetic field. It interacts with other magnets. The north end of a magnetized compass needle moves to line up with Earth's magnetic field.

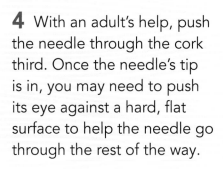

1 If your plastic container is taller than 3 inches (7.6 cm), have an adult help you cut its top off using a craft knife and scissors.

2 Have an adult use a large knife and cutting board to cut the **cork** into thirds. Save one third to use.

3 Next, magnetize the needle. Holding its eye, rub the needle lengthwise across the magnet in one direction. Repeat this sixty-five times.

4 With an adult's help, push the needle through the cork third. Once the needle's tip is in, you may need to push its eye against a hard, flat surface to help the needle go through the rest of the way.

5 Fill the container with water. Then drop in your compass. What happens? The needle's magnetized end should move to point north!

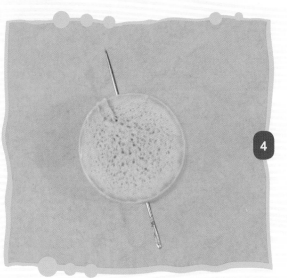

SCARF CORD KEEPER

Convert an old scarf into a cool roll-up case to keep track of your cords.

MATERIALS
~ repurposed scarf
~ roundhead fasteners
~ leftover felt pieces
~ ruler
~ scissors
~ glue
~ cords or earbuds

STEM Takeaway
Insulation protects the wires inside electrical cords. Rubber is a common insulator.

1 Fold the scarf in half, then in half again. Push a fastener through each corner. Fold the fastener ends flat.

2 Cut four 3 by 1 inch (7.6 by 2.5 cm) felt rectangles. Cut a small hole near each rectangle end.

3 Cut a felt rectangle as wide as one end of the scarf. This will be a pocket. Cut a small hole near each pocket corner and in the center of a long side. Attach the pocket to the scarf using fasteners in each hole. Glue the bottom and side edges of the pocket to the scarf.

4 Arrange the felt pieces from step 2 on the scarf and attach them using fasteners.

5 Wind up cords or earbuds and tuck them in the strips or pocket. Then roll up your scarf!

6 Cut a long, thin piece of felt and tie it around the scarf to hold the roll closed.

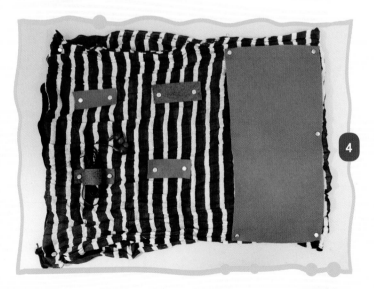

SWAP IT!
Swap felt for strips cut from an old T-shirt, blanket, or towel.

GLAM EARBUD MAKEOVER

Remodel and repair old but working earbuds or headphones with a colorful new look! Add earrings for flair.

MATERIALS
~ earbuds or headphones
~ electrical tape
~ craft glue
~ embroidery thread or string
~ old earrings
~ pliers
~ hot glue gun & glue sticks

STEM Takeaway
Earbud speakers rest inside the ear canal. This increases the intensity of the sounds coming from the speakers.

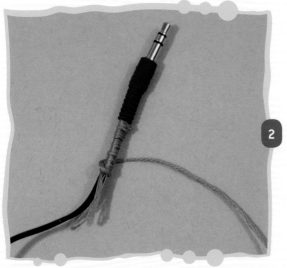

1 Locate any **frayed** or torn spots in the headphone or earbud wires. Wrap these areas in electrical tape.

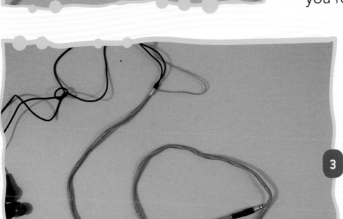

2 Place a dab of craft glue at the base of the wire. Tie the thread in a knot on top of the glue, then begin to wrap the thread around the wire. Wrap tightly enough to cover the wire completely.

3 Continue wrapping the wire until you reach its split. If the wires beyond this point are in good shape, skip ahead to step 5. If the separate speaker wires are frayed, go to step 4.

4 Wrap the thread up one wire. Add a dab of glue under the speaker, then knot and cut the thread. Tie the thread at the beginning of the second speaker wire and wrap the wire. Knot and glue down the end of the thread under the second speaker.

5 With an adult's help, use a pair of pliers to break the posts of the earrings. Hot glue the earrings to the back of the speakers.

EMOJI SUNDIAL

Sundials are ancient clocks. Use recycled materials to make your own sundial with a modern twist!

MATERIALS
~ recycled cardboard
~ scissors
~ paint
~ paintbrushes
~ craft knife or box cutter
~ sharpened pencil
~ hot glue gun & glue sticks
~ large rock

STEM Takeaway
The part of a sundial that casts a shadow is called a gnomon.

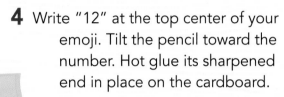

1 Cut a large circle from the cardboard and paint the shape.

2 Paint an emoji face on the circle.

3 In the center of the circle, have an adult make a small **slit** with a craft knife or box cutter. Insert the sharpened end of the pencil in the slit.

4 Write "12" at the top center of your emoji. Tilt the pencil toward the number. Hot glue its sharpened end in place on the cardboard.

5 On a sunny day, take your emoji outside and set it on a flat surface. Arrange the sundial so the pencil's shadow rests over the 12. Set a large rock on the dial to keep it from moving in wind. Return to the sundial on every hour until dusk and make a new mark on the dial where the pencil's shadow lands.

6 The sundial marks can change with the seasons. Reset your sundial each season by painting over the numbers and repeating step 5!

DIY DIGITAL FRAME

Construct a cardboard frame that turns a tablet or smartphone into a work of art!

MATERIALS
- tablet or smartphone
- recycled cardboard
- ruler
- pencil
- scissors
- craft knife
- glue
- various recycled decorative
- materials, such as paper towel tubes, beads, and straws
- paint
- paintbrushes

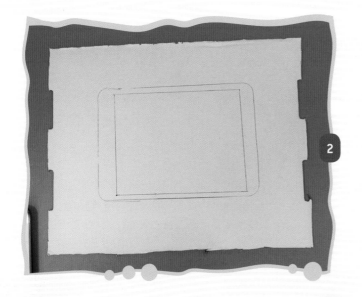

1 Trace the tablet or smartphone on cardboard.

2 Measure your device's screen. Draw a rectangle this size inside the traced shape.

3 Draw a 3-inch (7.6 cm) wide frame shape around the larger rectangle.

4 Cut around the outer edge of the frame with scissors.

DIY Digital Frame continued on next page

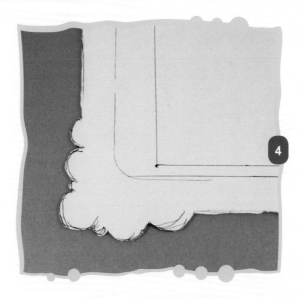

5 Have an adult use a craft knife to cut the screen-sized rectangle made in step 2 out of the frame.

6 Lay the frame so the traced shape is showing. This side is the back of the frame. Make a stand to attach to it. Cut a small rectangle and larger square out of cardboard. Glue these pieces together to make an L shape.

7 Glue the front edge of the L to the back of the frame. This creates a holder for the smartphone or tablet.

8 Once the glue dries on the back of the frame, decorate its front! Cut paper towel tubes into slices, curl them around a pencil, and glue them to the frame. Add beads, recycled cut-up straws, and more!

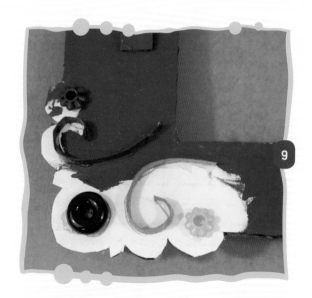

9 Paint the frame, including any added decorations.

10 Make props for the frame. Cut two right-angled triangles of the same size from cardboard.

11 Cut the triangles' top points off. Then cut a wide **notch** into each top. Glue the shapes' straight, vertical edges to the back of the frame.

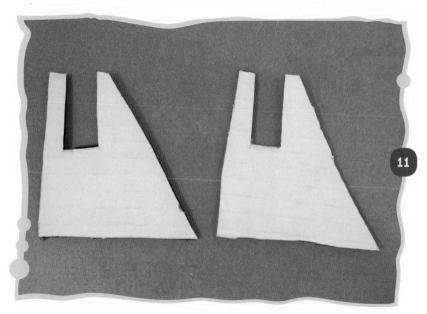

12 Download a free photo slideshow app and choose some photos to display in the app.

13 Rest your tablet or phone in the notches on the back of the frame when not in use. Enjoy your digital photo gallery!

PHONE CASE WALLET

Turn an old phone case and recycled materials into a wallet to hold money or odds and ends!

MATERIALS

~ thin plastic container or box with a flat side larger than the cell phone case
~ scissors
~ marker
~ old phone case
~ recycled gift tags or poster board
~ glue
~ old shirt, blanket, or leftover fabric
~ clear-drying craft glue
~ paintbrush
~ two small magnets

1 Cut out a large, flat side from the plastic container. Trace the phone case on the sheet and cut out the shape.

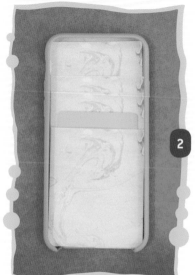

2 Cut the gift tags or poster board into rectangles as wide as the inside of the phone case. These will be wallet pockets. Glue the sides and bottom of each rectangle into the phone case, starting at the top. Overlap the pockets a bit.

3 Cut a square of fabric at least twice as wide as the phone case and lay it face down. Brush craft glue onto both sides of the plastic shape from step 1 and cover it in the fabric. Trim around the plastic. This is the wallet cover.

Phone Case Wallet continued on next page

4 Glue a scrap of fabric to the center of one long edge of the cover. Brush glue over the scrap and place a magnet inside. Fold the fabric over the magnet to make a tab. Trim any odd corners.

5 Cut a rectangle of fabric about half as large as the phone case. Glue one half to the long edge of the cover across from the tab.

6 Lay the phone case facedown on the cover. Fold and glue the other half of the fabric from step 5 to the back of the case.

7 Glue the second magnet along the open, long edge of the phone case.

8 Fill your wallet! To close it, press the case and cover together, then fold the magnet tab on top of the second magnet.

ODDS & ENDS

Craft materials and a little creativity can give new life to all kinds of old or recycled materials. What else can you repurpose?

LIGHT BULB

Turn a burned-out light bulb into a mini hot-air balloon! Paint the bulb to look like a balloon. Glue on string and a small paper cup to make a basket.

TOILET PAPER TUBE

Cut a wide notch into one side of a toilet paper tube and set a cell phone in it. Then play music! The tube will act as a stand and speaker.

CDS OR DVDS

Tie old CDs or DVDs together with string to make shiny garland!

CLOTH NAPKINS

Turn old cloth napkins into smartphone or tablet pouches! Fold and glue three corners together to form an envelope with an open flap. Tie a ribbon around the envelope to hold it closed.

KEYBOARD KEYS

Have an adult help you pop keyboard keys off a broken or non-working computer keyboard. Spell words or phrases with the keys and glue them to picture frames as captions.

GLOSSARY

accessories: small items worn with clothes or used with devices

cork: bark of the cork oak tree that is harvested and used as bottle stoppers or as insulation

creativity: the use of the imagination to think of new ideas

flair: a stylish or unique attractive quality

frayed: unraveled, worn, or shredded at the edges

insulation: material covering something in order to trap heat, electricity, or sound. This material is called an insulator.

intensity: the quality of being extreme in force, degree, or strength

navigate: to find where you are and where you need to go when traveling

notch: a V-shaped cut or nick on the edge of something

remodel: to change the structure of something

repurposing: giving a new purpose to something

revamp: to remake or redesign

slit: a straight, narrow cut or opening

technology: the use of scientific knowledge for practical purposes, such as machinery or equipment

transform: to completely change something

FURTHER INFORMATION

BOOKS

Challoner, Jack. *Maker Lab: 28 Super Cool Projects.*
New York: Dorling Kindersley, 2016. Find 28 step-by-step projects ranked by difficulty and made using everyday household materials.

Kenney, Karen Latchana. *Create Your Own Blog.*
Minneapolis: Lerner Publications, 2018. Follow a few simple steps to start your own blog, then share it with family and friends!

Leigh, Anna. *Design and Build Your Own Website.*
Minneapolis: Lerner Publications, 2018. Learn to create a real, working website featuring your favorite topics.

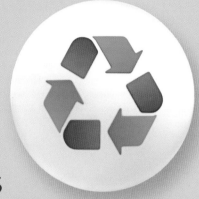

WEBSITES

AllCrafts: Computer Crafts
https://www.allcrafts.net/computer.htm
Find photos and free printable templates for fun projects you can make using a computer.

DIYs.com: Give Your Phone Case a Makeover with These 25 DIYs!
https://www.diys.com/customize-phone -cases/
These easy phone-case makeovers promise to take no longer than one afternoon!

Maker Education: Circuits and LED Projects
http://www.makereducation.com /circuits--led-projects.html
Browse tons of videos showing how to make cool tech projects that light up or move.

INDEX

ABOUT THE AUTHOR/ PHOTOGRAPHER

Veronica Thompson lives in a little brownstone in Brooklyn, New York, with her two puppies and wonderful husband. She spends her days crafting for her website, makescoutdiy.com, and building websites.